Guidelines for working with children with autistic spectrum disorders at Foundation Stage and Key Stage 1

Kathy Bache
Specialist Portage Home Visitor
South Gloucestershire Council

Eryl Daniels
SEN Support Network Manager
South Gloucestershire Council

Sally Hewison
Specialist Speech and Language Therapist
for children with complex communications needs
North Bristol NHS Trust

Paula Young
Pre-school Liaison Teacher
South Gloucestershire Council

Acknowledgements

We would like to thank colleagues from the Early Years Inclusion Team (Inclusion Support Service), Educational Psychology Service and Speech and Language Therapy Service for their support with the preparation of these guidelines. Also thanks to Ambourne House, Frome Opportunity Group and Foot Prints Pre-school for providing photographs of an appropriate environment and visual aids to support children with an ASD.

Guidelines for Working with Children with an ASD at Foundation Stage and KS1

Contents

Foreword

What is an ASD?	1
Implications of an ASD	2
Roles and responsibilities	4
Making sense of their behaviour - The STAR approach	5
How can you help?	8
Transitions	12
Where can you get help?	14

Foreword

The Education Service has recognised that there is a need for specific advice to support early years practitioners working with children with an autistic spectrum disorder (ASD) in pre-school and school settings and therefore, with colleagues from North Bristol NHS Trust, has produced these guidelines. The guidelines have been written to help colleagues develop a greater understanding of ASD and to support the early identification and provision for children in their earliest years as outlined in *Together from the Start* DFES (2003) and *Sure Start Guidance* (2003). Children with an ASD bring to early years settings qualities unique to them, which should be valued and, where possible, accommodated.

Van Krevelen (cited in Wing 1991) noted that the low-functioning child with autism 'lives in a world of his own,' whereas the higher functioning child with autism 'lives in our world, but in his own way.'

We hope that a greater understanding of differences in learning styles and social interaction will promote effective inclusion and that all staff carrying out an invaluable role working with young children with an ASD find these guidelines helpful.

Jane Spouse

Jane C. Spouse

Deputy Director for Children and Young People

Wing, L (1991) Language, Social and Cognitive Impairments in Autism and Severe Mental Retardation, *Journal of Autism and Developmental Disorders Vol 11*

What is an autistic spectrum disorder?

Autistic spectrum disorder (ASD) is a complex developmental disability that lasts throughout life. It affects more boys than girls and includes the syndromes described by Kanner and Asperger.

ASD affects the way a person communicates, relates to people and understands the world around them. These difficulties are referred to as 'the triad of impairments'. For a diagnosis to be made, specific types and degrees of difference must be present in each of the three areas:

- social interaction
- social communication
- flexibility of thought.

Children with autism vary greatly, as the effects of autism can be mild or severe and be influenced by age, personality, life experiences and any other disability the child may have. Most children with Kanner syndrome will have moderate or severe learning difficulties and up to half may not learn to use spoken language. Those with Asperger syndrome have fewer problems with language and are less likely to have additional learning difficulties, although they often experience problems with communication and motor skills.

Most children with Asperger syndrome attend a mainstream setting and school. As a result of the core differences, the problems with motor skills and unusual responses to sensory stimuli, children with Asperger syndrome often experience a range of significant difficulties in school. However, children with Asperger syndrome can also have considerable strengths, eg a good memory for facts, exceptional concentration for activities of their choice, particular interests, favourite toys or video, or may recite 'chunks' from a story or dialogue from a video.

Due to the wide variation in the difficulties experienced within settings or schools, there has to be a corresponding variation in the provision made for children with an ASD. Some require no additional support or resources whilst others may have a Statement of Special Educational Need and have a variety of different types and amounts of support.

The guidance within this booklet should help you to understand the individual needs and behaviour of children with an ASD, as well as to tailor the support provided for each individual. *Many of the strategies that have proved effective in helping children with an ASD, may also help other children who are experiencing difficulties with relation to social, organisation and communication skills.*

Implications of an ASD for children in the Foundation Stage

Each of the three areas of difference – social interaction, social communication and flexibility of thought – has implications for a child's ability to be included in all aspects of school life.

Social interaction
Children who have an ASD will have difficulties interpreting and using the unwritten rules of social interaction. This means that pupils will have difficulty understanding the intent of peers and adults at school and often misinterpret body language.

For example:
Children with an ASD may wish to have friends and to mix socially with their peers. Children may appear to be on the edge of social groups. However, because of social misunderstandings they may behave in an inappropriate way. For example, they may ask questions such as 'Why are you fat?' Other children with an ASD may be very isolated.

Children with an ASD may appear to tolerate peers and play in parallel with them. Large group situations can be stressful. A child with an ASD may hide their face, cover ears, talk out of context, or hum if others are sitting too close.

Children with an ASD may have difficulty with empathy and so find it difficult to recognise how another person is feeling.

Social communication
Children with an ASD will have different communication skills to others. This may range from little or no spoken language to a child with a sophisticated adult-like style.

They may have a speech style that does not fit into the social context of the community. Some pupils may have unusual intonation, for example, an 'American' accent, or very flat prosody ('monotonous').

Children with an ASD have difficulties with non-verbal interactions. Children may have difficulties with turn-taking in conversation, eye gaze, body language, and proximity. Children with an ASD may talk repetitively about their own particular interests.

Some children may use jargon or chunks of language repeated from familiar situations e.g. a favourite video. Other children may echo language used by others. This may be a sign that the child does not understand.

For example:
When asked where they went on holiday, a child with an ASD might give a detailed description of all the roads and signposts passed, but not share the name of the town.

Some children with an ASD have difficulty understanding spoken language. This might be because they have language difficulties and do not understand concepts or grammar or may have difficulty remembering language. Other pupils may have difficulty identifying when language is addressed to them, so they find it very difficult to screen out all the language that they do not need to process.

Children with an ASD who do have good language skills will usually have difficulty using language for reasoning, eg predicting.

More able children with Asperger syndrome may have unexpectedly good mechanical reading skills. Their understanding of language may not match their reading or language skill (hyperlexia).

Flexibility of thought (imagination/play)
Changes to the usual routine can cause anxiety. Children with an ASD usually have limited play skills. They may re-enact familiar stories, e.g. from a favourite story or video, but will usually find it very difficult to allow another child to get involved in the play.

Children may not respond to the same motivators as their peers. Many children are not motivated by the teacher's praise but might be more motivated by a concrete system that results in a preferred activity, eg time with a particular toy, or a sticker relating to their topic of interest.

Sensory – motor issues
Many children with an ASD are hypersensitive to sensory stimuli. This can be touch, sound, taste, smell and/or sight. This may result in apparently inappropriate responses to ordinary stimuli.

For example:
Children may refuse to go in a particular classroom or toilets as they find the smell unbearable.

Children may scream or cover their ears when they hear a whiteboard pen 'squeak' on the whiteboard.

Children might seek out a particular position in the classroom where the light reflects on a shiny surface and look at this through their fingers.

Children may be physically sick if they are expected to eat a particular food due to the taste, texture and/or smell.

Children may find some sensations unbearable, including labels on clothes or someone touching them.

The playground may be overwhelmingly noisy for some pupils.

Children with an ASD may be easily distracted due to heightened awareness of sensory stimuli. Other distractions could be their own thought processes related to topic of particular interest and/or lack of the awareness of their membership of the class group.

Some children with an ASD have good motor skills, but many others have motor co-ordination difficulties.

Roles and responsibilities – who can help?

A pupil with an ASD may be known to a number of agencies. For example:

SENCO	A teacher/early years practitioner who co-ordinates work with children who have special educational needs in the school/early years setting
Portage Worker	Home-based pre-school education for children with significant Special Educational Needs
Speech/Language Therapist (SLT)	Works with children who have problems with understanding, communicating and speaking.
Paediatrician	Doctor for babies/children
Educational Psychologist	Trained to help children and young people experiencing difficulties in learning and/or behaviour
Early Years Inclusion Support	A teacher with experience of special educational needs in early years employed by the education authority to advise, support and help settings meet the needs of individual children and to liaise with parents and health professionals
Area SENCO	Support non-maintained early years settings with SEN management. Support may be provided to individual children with SEN referred by pre-schools
Health Visitor	A nurse who advises on general child health, particular problems and monitor's progress
School Nurse	Gives advice and support to school aged children, their parents/carers and teachers on any health issues.

Other services may occasionally be involved with a particular child/family.

Social Services	Assess child's and family's need for services. Provide advice and support.
Occupational Therapist	Help children become as independent as possible in everyday activities such as personal care, eating and drinking, play and school work. Employed by health or social services.

These staff may be able to provide specific advice to the setting to support the child.

The staff working in the school or pre-school setting are responsible for the day to day implementation of the strategies suggested by these agencies.

Making sense of the children's behaviour

It is important to make detailed observations of children with ASD. From your observations, you will gain a clear picture of the children's strengths and needs. The observations will help you know the children, to recognise what has a positive effect and what creates a negative response. Observe the children in various situations such as free play, group times, adult directed activities and observe social interactions. Base observations on the triad of differences – social interaction, social communication and imagination and play. This will help to focus your attention. When making observations these are some key questions to ask yourself.

When observing communication, do they:

1 vocalise?
2 produce speech?
3 use another person's body or hand as a tool?
4 understand speech or accept the attempts of others to communicate with them?
5 request something with a gesture?
6 request something using a pointing gesture?
7 bring something to another person just to show them?
8 point something out to another person to share attention?
9 have a sound or gesture for refusal?
10 wave bye-bye or clap hands?

When observing social interaction, do they:

1 look at an object when it has been shown or are aware that they have to share attention?
2 take turns during a social routine?
3 show interest in other children?
4 show appropriate emotions at other people's actions?
5 do they calm at physical reassurance from a familiar person (cuddle)?
6 how do they react to being separated from parent/carer?

When observing imagination and play, do they:

1 enjoy peek a boo games? Do they take part or do they just watch?
2 enjoying playing with an adult? For example taking part in a familiar song or nursery rhyme
3 do they use simple actions with an object? (This could be mouthing, tapping or spinning)
4 do they know that rings go on poles, bricks go on top of each other and toys go in containers?
5 do they show any pretend play? Is it role play, imaginative play or merely imitation of things they have seen at home?

What are they trying to communicate? What is happening?
Observing in this way will aid planning of activities for children with an ASD. You will have a clearer understanding of the children's communication, social interaction and play skills that will help you to think of the children's developmental needs.

STAR
Setting Trigger Actions Results

Setting
Environmental – large noisy busy free play session.
Personal – the child is involved in his favourite activity, he is calm and in a world of his own.

Triggers
The teacher tells him it is tidy up time, 'Put the toy away in the box.'

Action (the behaviour)
The child becomes upset and runs up and down the room,

Result
The teacher directs him to the box but he becomes upset, runs and shrieks.

What is happening?
The function of the action was to express that he wanted to continue playing with a toy.

To change the behaviour the adult can alter the settings, manipulate the trigger or teach an alternative action.
Alter the triggers by using a visual clue to show that the activity should end. This gives the child time to prepare for a change of activity. Examples of visual clues include a picture of what will happen next or a timer with a countdown to end of activity.

STAR Approach

Date:

Settings	Triggers	Actions

How can you help?

These tips are ways of working with children with an ASD.
Not all are appropriate for every child. You need to get to know them.

Use parents – they are the experts on their own children.

Many of these tips will benefit all children.

Structure

Children with an ASD can find it difficult to make sense of what is going on around them, find life confusing and so experience high levels of anxiety.

Remember: anxiety presents as challenging or inappropriate behaviour.

Children with an ASD like routine and structure. The more predictable the learning environment, the more likely it is that they will cope with learning and social demands and be less likely to experience anxiety. Reducing anxiety enables the children to learn better.

Tips

Physical environment

- Think about the layout of the room — furniture, equipment and toys

- Organise the room into distinct areas that guide the children to know what is expected of them. This helps a child with an ASD to make sense of what is happening

- If possible provide boundaries or signs to make clear the different areas for the different activities, eg the use of suspended hoops with pictures to show the activity for that table or to show role-play area

- Organise the storage of equipment/toys by labelling or colour coding boxes or shelves

- Be aware that some children with an ASD are hypersensitive to stimuli: light, noise, touch, smell, heat

- When possible provide a quiet area to which the child may withdraw to complete a task, work 1:1 with an adult or work with a partner supported by an adult. This could be a table in the corner of the room, facing a wall free of posters and distractions.

- If the room is too busy or overcrowded, look to see if a quiet area for tasks can be provided elsewhere. This could also be used as a 'sanctuary' when children are highly anxious, eg hypersensitivity to noise or movement or finds it difficult to cope with the demand of a learning activity. A beanbag placed in a quiet corner can be helpful.

- Think about where and how children sit for certain activities, eg story or snack time. Give them seating places so that everyone knows where to sit. If necessary, provide children with an ASD with a seating mat on which to sit.

- Observe the child to determine a favourite toy/object, then place it out of reach but still visible to the child. When the child wants the toy/object he will need to communicate to an adult what he wants, either non-verbally or verbally.

People

- Consider the adults working in your setting to determine who shows empathy and is supportive to children, so that interactions between adult and children are positive.

- Think about the pairing and grouping of children. Choose a suitable peer who befriends the child and would provide a positive model of behaviour and communication.

- Use adult role-play to demonstrate appropriate behaviour in situations and to model the use of toys/equipment.

Order of session

Remember, providing a predictable learning environment reduces anxiety.

- Establish and maintain routines –
  - arrival
  - opening activities
  - snack time
  - going to the toilet
  - closing activities
  - departure.

- All adults should try to be consistent with routines and in ways of working with children with ASD.

- When possible, pre-warn children with ASD of changes to routines. Anticipate any difficulties and explain changes to children with ASD. Be clear about what will happen during the session.

Order of activity/task

- Make explicit how to complete a learning activity/task, eg painting, sand play or going to the toilet. Then maintain that routine.

- Structure activity into small steps:
  - what to do
  - when
  - with whom
  - where
  - when activity is finished
  - what to do next.

- Give warning of when to stop an activity and use a signal to show that it is time to stop, eg a bell, musical instrument or clapping.

- Structure a learning task into small steps. Again, be clear about what to do, where to start, how much and when task is finished.

- Provide a start work tray of one colour and a finished work tray of another colour. As tasks are completed, the child can progress from one tray to the other.

- If necessary, teach the steps of an activity/task one at a time, starting with the last step first. The child is then always rewarded for completing the activity/task.

Visuals

Use photographs, pictures, drawings or symbols to make visual aids. Younger children and those experiencing difficulties relate better to objects or photographs but do ensure that you gain parental permission to use photographs.

Tips

The order of the session

- A visual timetable supports children's understanding and provides a record of what is happening throughout the session. It takes away the reliance upon understanding language and this helps to reduce anxiety. Children gain in confidence by seeing what to expect and what to do.

- Display a visual timetable for all the children to see.

- Sometimes it is also necessary to provide the child with ASD with a copy of the timetable.

- Timetables can run from left to right or top to bottom.

- Initially an adult should run through the timetable with the child with ASD and refer to it throughout the session.

The order of an activity/task

- A visual work schedule shows children what to do and helps them to develop positive work routines.

- It can show them the structure of a task, leading them through it step by step to the finish. Pictures can be removed as the child progresses through the task. This gives positive reinforcement.

- It can show that the completion of an adult–directed activity/task leads to reward, reinforcing the teaching of 'first work, then play.'

Order of an activity/task
How to get dressed

How to get ready for snack time

Expectations about behaviour
How to listen, how to play.

Choice board to select activity
I want sand

Label equipment and toys

Language

Children with an ASD can present with a range of language ability, from having no verbal language to quite sophisticated language. All children with an ASD experience difficulties with understanding and the social use of language.

Tips

- Adults should reduce their language when giving information or instruction — Keep It Short and Simple (KISS).

- Be specific — say exactly what you mean, eg instead of 'Can you tidy away the Lego' say 'Put Lego in box' or 'Lego, box.' Say what you want the child to do, eg 'hands on knees' rather than 'sit still' or 'don't fidget.'

- Structure situations or activities to promote communication, eg the placement of a toy out of reach so that the child has to request it through gesture or speech.

- Use the child's interests and join in his play. Sit alongside and share the activity. Gradually involve another child in the activity and introduce turn taking.

- Model language and comment on the play but keep your language simple.

- Avoid non-literal language, eg 'hang on a minute' or 'pull yourself together.'

- Say child's name and pause before instruction to give time to process information, eg 'Name_____ instruction.'

- Use visual aids to support understanding of instructions.

- Ask simple direct questions and wait. Give child time to process language and respond: OWL — Observe, Wait and Listen (Hanen Programme).

- If repetition is necessary, use the same language, unless it definitely needs simplification. Otherwise the child has to start processing the language again from the beginning.

- Many children require high levels of repetition to learn new vocabulary.

- Be consistent in the use of language for key times/activities in the session. For example, if you agreed to use the term toilet, then do not confuse by using other terms such as loo or bathroom.

- Talk to parents about the language used at home. Find out what the parents say.

- Some children are helped by hearing alternatives, for example, 'apple or banana,' rather than open ended questions such as 'What do you want to eat?'

- Accept their communication. For example, reinforce but do not correct if the child says 'nana.' Model *banana* or *I want a banana* and give it to the child. Do not insist that the child repeats what you have said.

Transitions

Tips to support transitions

Experience has shown that the importance of a well-planned transition not only for children with ASD. This applies to whatever level of transition, for example pre-school to Reception, year 1 to year 2 and so on.

Early co-operation and extra preparation for children with ASD help staff to develop successful strategies and structures within their classrooms. Staff can become more familiar with the child and their needs before induction days and draw on the knowledge of those who already know the child well.

Supporting transition prior to leaving pre-school

- Contact between pre-schools and a school is essential early in the summer term. Pre-schools are very keen to develop links and support a successful transition into Reception.

- Involve school staff as early as possible by arranging to visit the pre-school setting. Observe children: discuss strategies that work and *don't* work with particular children. What is the pre-school doing successfully that the school can continue? Look at Individual Play Plans and observations, talk to the setting SENCO and value what the staff have done for the child. With parental permission they will willingly share information.

- Talk to the parents! What strategies/language is the child familiar with at home? Would the, be appropriate to use in class? Does the child have particular sensitivities such as sound, food, touch, smell, sleep difficulties etc.?

- How did the child settle into pre-school? Were any particular strategies required that could support the move into school?

- Pre-schools invite the school to attend any reviews for specific children held during the summer term.

- Staff should seek training if necessary to increase their skills.

- Many children with a diagnosis of ASD are likely to be known to a number of agencies. The Pre-school Liaison Teachers will also contact the school early in the summer term to discuss transition for those children known to themselves or other members of the Early Years Team. Parents will often approach staff.

- Plan additional visit days for children with ASD before planned induction days. Pre-schools are often keen to support these and will send a member of their staff who the child knows and trusts to accompany them. This may need to be outside school hours – depends on the individual child.

- Use a digital camera and take photographs of the child in a new setting – for example in the class entrance area, hall, classroom areas, dining areas, playground or office etc.

- Provide photographs of staff members who would have immediate contact with the child – teacher, LSA, head, secretary.

- Use these photographs to make a book to share with the child in plenty of time before they start. Parents can continue this throughout the summer break and the child then knows a little more about what to expect.

Supporting transition into school:

- Seek advice from all agencies involved. Make sure any contact names/numbers are recorded on file.

- Consider the school induction programme – is it more appropriate for the child to attend every morning rather than changing each day/week? This needs to be discussed with parents and balanced against the change of peer group which would result, with careful planning and clear warnings to the child about changes of routine and the need for the child to learn the afternoon routine.

- A visual timetable should be ready for use from the first summer induction day and prominently displayed **at the child's eye level.**

- The child's attention needs to be directed to using the visual timetable. Picture support should be appropriate – does the child use photos or symbols? This may be beneficial to other children too.

- Any other visual aids should be ready and clearly explained to all children and staff from the first day.

- If the class is divided, both halves of the class need to know the other exists! It is often a flashpoint when the two halves come together, so use discussion and photographs of the other half.

- Give clear warnings of any change *before* it happens to the whole group. The child with ASD may need a quiet prompt of their own.

- Keep your language simple – *reduce* it to its basics to provide clear instructions.

- Gradually introduce a child with ASD to echoey areas such as the hall for PE or long assemblies. Consider very carefully whether it is really necessary for children with ASD to attend assembly times which are often distressing for them.

- Take small groups of two or three children around the playground areas so boundaries are clearly explained. Extra marking may be necessary. For example, highlight lines with bright spray paint.

Where can you get help……..

Should you need or want to know more, consider the following:

For further advice contact the Educational Psychology Service or Early Years Inclusion Team via the Area SENCO who may then involve other external agencies such as Speech and Language Therapy Service.

Look in the Training Booklet for Early Years Carers, Playworkers, School Staff and Parents

Contact The National Autistic Society (NAS)
393 City Road,
London
EC1V 1NG

Tel. 020 7833 2299
Helpline 0845 070 4004   autismhelpline@nas.org.uk

Useful websites

www.autism.org.uk   www.info.autism.org.uk   www.autismuk.com
www.dotolearn.com

Practical strategies

***Cumine V, Leach J and Stevenson G (2000)** *Autism in the early years.*
London, David Fulton
***Hannah, L (2001)** *Teaching young children with autistic spectrum disorders to learn: a practical guide for parents and staff in mainstream schools and nurseries.*
London: The National Autistic Society
***Jordan, R (2002)** *Autistic spectrum disorders in the early years, a guide for practitioners.* Lichfield, Qed
***Leicester City Council (1998)** *Autism – how to help your young child.*
London, NAS
***Leicester City Council and Leicestershire County Council (1998)**
Asperger syndrome – practical strategies for the classroom: a teacher's guide.
London: The National Autistic Society
***Whitaker, P (2001)** *Challenging behaviour and autism: making sense – making progress.* London: The National Autistic Society

Communication skills: resources for small group work

Schroeder A (2001) *Time to talk.* Wisbech, LDA

Delamain C and Spring J (2000) *Developing baseline communication skills.* Bicester, Winslow

Delamain C and Spring J (2003) *Speaking, listening and understanding.* Speechmark Publishing Ltd, Birmingham

Booklets

* **Prithvi, P (2005)** Classroom and playground. London: The National Autistic Society

*Available from NAS Publications
Tel 020 7033 9237
Fax 020 7739 0479
Or order online at www.autism.org.uk/pubs